MW00615775

IMAGES
of America

PAGOSA SPRINGS

The *Guinness Book of World Records* awarded the Springs Resort & Spa in Pagosa Springs the world record for the deepest geothermal hot springs measured by a plumb line; however, it is still unknown how deep the spring is. During the official measuring for the award, a 1,002-foot-long plumb line was used, but it ran out before reaching the bottom. Southern Ute Heritage Dancers and Miss Southern Ute Sage Rohde are pictured here at the awards ceremony. (Courtesy of the *Southern Ute Drum*, photographer Jeremy Wade Shockley.)

ON THE COVER: The school marching band entry is seen in the 1950s Fourth of July parade. Familiar town businesses, including Hersch's Mercantile, Pagosa Hardware, Jackish Drug, and the Pagosa Hotel and Café, form the backdrop for this patriotic event. The town's annual Fourth of July celebration historically was, and still is, the biggest celebration in town every year. An uncropped version of this image appears on page 103. (Courtesy of the Harman estate.)

IMAGES
of America

PAGOSA SPRINGS

Kristin Bowen

ARCADIA
PUBLISHING

Copyright © 2020 by Kristin Bowen
ISBN 978-1-4671-0526-2

Published by Arcadia Publishing
Charleston, South Carolina

Printed in the United States of America

Library of Congress Control Number: 2020932848

For all general information, please contact Arcadia Publishing:
Telephone 843-853-2070
Fax 843-853-0044
E-mail sales@arcadiapublishing.com
For customer service and orders:
Toll-Free 1-888-313-2665

Visit us on the Internet at www.arcadiapublishing.com

This book is dedicated to my Mom, my biggest fan.

CONTENTS

ACKNOWLEDGMENTS

Photographs were used with permission from the Western History and Genealogy Department of the Denver Public Library and the Library of Congress. *Pagosa Springs Sun* articles were used many times as a source of information. The Goodman family kindly shared Goodman's Department Store history and photographs for use in the book. The San Juan National Forest (SJNF) and the Colorado Department of Transportation (CDOT) allowed use of their photographs, and their staff Mark Roper (SJNF) and Lauren Cooper and Hannah Braun (CDOT) generously assisted me in my search for images. I would like to thank Alden Naranjo, tribal historian at the Southern Ute Indian Tribe, for sharing knowledge that only you could provide. Thanks are owed to Jen Rumore for granting access to the Harman family collection and to J.R. Ford for enabling access to the R.D. Hott collection—the book could not have become a reality without you. Photographs were used from the archives at Fort Lewis College, Center of Southwest Studies, and the La Plata County Historical Society, and their staffs were extremely helpful. Dean Cox provided me with photographs and more and deserves a special thank-you for all his help and willingness to share his knowledge and love of this area. I also thank the Community United Methodist Church, Archuleta School District, Franklin Anderson, Ben Lynch, the Elliot family, and Junior, Flo, and Paul Gallegos for your generous assistance and use of your photographs. My gratitude is given to Jamie Miller, owner of Feather Your Nest antique store; Ray Martinez, owner of Ray's Hair Care; Deborah Archuleta; and Selah Mountain Pharmacy for letting me use materials for this book. Thanks are given to the *Southern Ute Drum* and Jeremy Wade Shockley for providing the frontispiece image. Also, thanks are given to Richard Smith, Matt Simons, Cassandra Atencio, Dr. Jeffrey Blythe, and Randy Green for information and assistance during this project. Last but not least, special thanks go to my children Cooper and Oakley for their love and belief in me.

INTRODUCTION

The Pagosa area was the traditional homeland of the Ute people, but it was also used by other currently recognized Native American tribes, namely the Navajo and the Jicarilla Apache. Studies of archaeological sites at Chimney Rock, what is now the Navajo Reservoir area, and the Piedra River drainage have identified remnants of populations from the Pueblo I (750–900 CE) and Pueblo II (900–1150 CE) time periods. Chimney Rock represents one of the largest Pueblo II communities in Southwestern Colorado and is considered a Chacoan cultural outlier. By the 1200s, however, these early residents of the region had migrated south toward the pueblos of the Rio Grande.

The Utes called themselves *Nuche*, which means "Mountain People." The Ute believe that they have been in their territory since time immemorial. They traveled over a large territory in an annual cycle, moving to areas when the plants or animals there were available to be harvested. They would summer in the high country for its myriad resources and then return to the lower valleys in the winter. Ute traditional territory extended across much of what is now Colorado, Utah, and Northern New Mexico. The Ute were the earliest Western tribes to acquire horses, and they incorporated these animals fully into their culture. With this lifestyle change, they extended their territory of trading, raiding, and hunting areas into Arizona, Wyoming, Nebraska, Kansas, Oklahoma, and Texas.

Hispanic settlement of the Chama River valley (south of here in what is now New Mexico) began in 1765. Settlements spread to the Abique area by the 1740s, and they continued to spread north. The Pagosa Springs area was part of Mexico prior to the Treaty of Guadalupe Hidalgo, which ended the Mexican War in 1848. By the 1800s, Spanish families had started moving into the San Juan area.

The first European explorers entered the northern San Juan region in the 1700s. Juan Antonio María de Rivera's first expedition of 1765 traveled from Abiquiu, New Mexico, to Piedra Parada, which is today known as Chimney Rock, and from there, explored Southwestern Colorado. Rivera was the one who named the region's rivers, including the Navajo, San Juan, Piedra, Pinos, Florida, Animas, and Dolores. On August 5, 1776, the Dominguez and Escalante expedition passed through what would become Pagosa Junction and continued west through what became Arboles, Allison, and Tiffany. The old Native American trails that the Dominguez and Escalante expedition used were then used as early trade routes from Santa Fe to California and were later called the Old Spanish Trail. The Old Spanish Trail was designated by Congress as a national historic trail in 2002.

In search of a new route from Santa Fe to Utah, the government sponsored the US Army Corps of Topographical Engineers expedition of 1859. Led by Capt. John N. Macomb, the expedition retraced some of the route of the Old Spanish Trail and resulted in the first documented visit to Pagosa Springs. In his 1859 report, Macomb wrote of visiting the hot springs, calling it by the Ute name, Pah-gosa, which translates to stinky water. Worn trails from all directions converged on the springs when they were first observed, and Macomb figured that while the springs had never been seen by the whites, they were well known among the natives.

Extensive European interest in the San Juan region began with gold exploration in Southwestern Colorado between 1859 and 1861. Gold was discovered in 1860 in Bakers Park, now Silverton, by prospector Charles Baker. Subsequently, Baker constructed a toll road from Baker City to Abiquiu to get the ore out; in 1861, this became the first road to go through Pagosa.

Pagosa hot springs was officially taken by the government in 1868. A reservation that covered almost one third of Colorado was established for the Ute, and its boundary was drawn just south of the springs. In 1873, after gold and silver were discovered in the San Juan Mountains, the Brunot Agreement was created. The agreement severely shrunk Ute lands, opening 6,000 more acres of former Ute land.

In 1877, President Hayes set aside a one-square-mile area around the hot springs as a townsite for future development. In 1878, the US Army started building a post on the west bank of the San Juan River to control the Ute and to protect settlers from escalating conflicts with them. It was originally proposed as a cantonment, then a camp, and finally a fort, named Fort Lewis, all in quick succession. By this time, approximately 100 early settlers had already set up here, a post office had been established, and the area's first sawmill was cutting boards in preparation for the Army's arrival. A six-mile-square area around the original one-mile townsite was declared a military reservation in 1879.

The new community was looking forward to growth as it was on the wagon road connecting Santa Fe to Silverton and had the security of an Army post as well as the draw of the healing springs. Homesteaders came to ranch and farm, entrepreneurs started businesses to serve the new residents, and Pagosa Springs seemed destined for development. However, things quickly turned the other direction after the "Meeker Massacre" in 1879 in Northwestern Colorado, which prompted the Army to move the fort to Hesperus as the Pagosa area was determined to be too remote. The name Fort Lewis was reassigned to the new post, and the Pagosa post was officially abandoned in 1882.

In 1876, Welch Nossaman built the first cabin near the hot springs. The story goes that the Ute burned it down, he rebuilt, it was burned again, and this cycle continued for several years. Public facilities could not be built as it was federally owned land reserved for the purposes of the military reservation. However, that did not stop Thomas Blair (of Blair Street in Silverton notoriety) from constructing the first bathhouse next to the springs in 1881 (on government land). The town of Pagosa Springs was platted and surveyed in 1883.

The region was originally part of Conejos County, one of the original 17 counties of Colorado. State senator Antonio D. Archuleta introduced a bill to separate a new county from Conejos County, which, subsequently, was named Archuleta County after him and his family when it was formed in 1885.

An 1890 act was passed by Congress to open the former Pagosa Springs Military Reservation lands to the public for homestead entry. In 1891, the town was incorporated, and it remains the only incorporated town in Archuleta County. By this time, many of the businesses had moved over to the west side of the river to occupy the area that was abandoned by Fort Lewis. Homesteading was well established by 1899, and growth throughout the region was triggered by an increasing dependency on an agricultural economy.

In the 1890s, newspapers were being printed, gas streetlights were installed in town, and a telephone was built between Pagosa Springs and the lumber town of Edith. Local chapters of fraternal organizations, such as the Freemasons and the International Order of Odd Fellows, were formed, as well as women's organizations such as the Rebekahs and the Women of Woodcraft. Several denominations of church services were being held in various places while congregations raised money to construct church buildings. Early settlers hoped a large resort would end up developing in Pagosa, hence the 1890s advertisements dubbing it "the Carlsbad of America," which referred to the spa town in the Czech Republic. In the early 1900s, this phrase alluded to the prestigious European spa tradition.

One

1870s–1890s

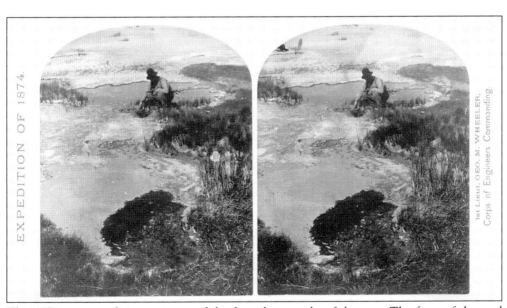

This 1874 stereograph image is one of the first photographs of the area. The front of the card reads, "Expedition of 1874 1st Lieut. Geo. M. Wheeler, Corps of Engineers Commanding." The back identifies the subject: "One of the group of Pagosa Hot Springs, showing incrustations on the surface. Much prized by the Indians and miners on account of supposed healing qualities. Principal mineral element, Sulphate of Soda." (Courtesy of the Library of Congress.)

This is part of another set of stereograph images from the expedition of 1874. Stereographic images present two off-set images separately to the left and right eyes. The images were mounted on a card and then looked at through a hand-held viewer, giving the illusion of three-dimensional depth. (Courtesy of the Library of Congress.)

This image, taken by photographer Timothy H. O'Sullivan during the expedition of 1874, is likely the first photograph of a person bathing in the springs. The main spring was always too hot to touch, but other smaller pools could be bathed in. This photograph and others are grouped under the label "Explorations and surveys west of 100th meridian at the Library of Congress." (Courtesy of the Library of Congress.)

This extremely rare 1881 photograph shows the original Fort Lewis buildings prior to the town of Pagosa Springs. The fort did not last long here, and in January 1881, the new Fort Lewis in Hesperus was designated. Some soldiers were left to guard the government buildings that had been left behind, but by November 1882, the fort was officially abandoned. (Courtesy of the La Plata County Historical Society.)

This postcard features a sketch of Fort Lewis at Pagosa Springs in 1880. An X has been drawn on top of one of the fort's log buildings on the left with a line connecting to text that notes which house the sender had lived in. Some of the fort buildings were disassembled by the Army and moved to the new fort, but some were left in place, and many settlers resided in them when they first moved to town. (Courtesy of Fort Lewis College, Center of Southwest Studies.)

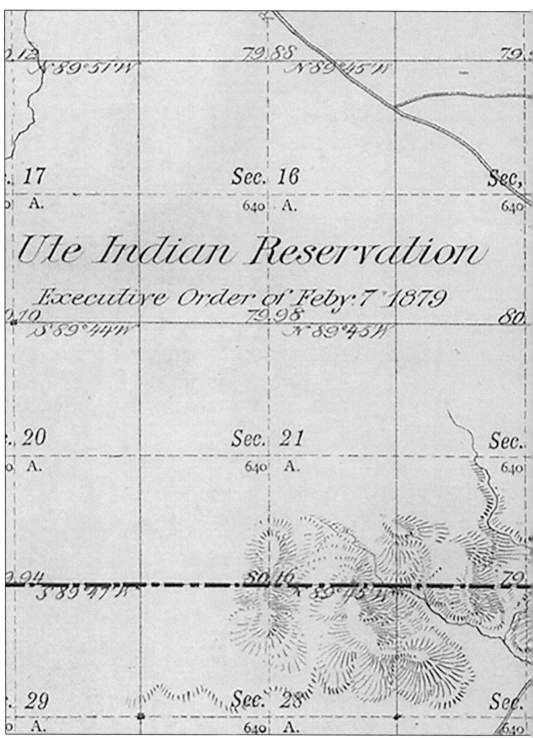

This 1881 survey plat map of Pagosa shows how the town was surrounded by the Ute Indian Reservation as designated in 1879. In the center of the townsite is the location of the Valentine Scrip that Henry Foote filed in 1875, which centered on the hot springs. Scrip was a certificate

from the land office granting private ownership of pieces of public lands resulting from a trial of claims before the courts; the Valentine Scrip resulted from a disputed land title fight in California by Thomas Bishop Valentine. (Courtesy of General Land Office Records.)

A group of Ute on horseback is pictured in 1905. Tribal families' oral histories say the Southern Ute Moache and Capote bands acquired horses from the Spanish as early as the 1590s. The Ute began to let the Spanish settle in select parts of their territory, present-day Colorado, as they benefitted from this relationship since the Spanish had access to goods that they wanted. Metal tools and weapons were highly desired; for example, cooking food in a metal pot compared to a ceramic pot or basket was a huge change. (Courtesy of the Library of Congress.)

Buckskin Charley is seen wearing the Indian Peace Medal that he was given by Pres. Benjamin Harrison in 1890 for helping keep good relations between the Southern Ute and the US government. Buckskin Charley was the last hereditary chief of the Southern Utes, who served that role for 56 years. After his death, his son Antonio Buck Sr. became the first elected chairman of the Southern Ute Indian Tribe. (Courtesy of the Library of Congress.)

Ute men are in ceremonial dress in front of tepees by the river north of Ignacio. On horseback are, from left to right, Edwin Cloud, Buckskin Charley, unidentified, Antonio Buck Sr., Pe-ve-ge, Nanice, and Severo. (The person standing is unidentified.) Buckskin Charley was chief of the Muache band starting in 1870. Severo was chief of the Capote band. The Ute had previously constructed temporary shelters called wickiups and transitioned into living in tepees after they acquired the horse, as the horse could drag the long tepee poles when they moved from place to place. (Courtesy of the Library of Congress.)

A more modern photograph, taken by Mark Roper, shows an example of what is referred to now as a culturally scarred tree. These trees found in the forests of Colorado are lasting evidence of the Ute use of the area. The Ute would peel long strips of bark off the ponderosa pines for the softer inner bark called cambium, which they used for food and medicine. The scars date from the early to late 1800s. (Courtesy of the San Juan National Forest.)

The 1881 survey plat map of the Pagosa Springs placer mining claim of Byron Roberts et al. was 80 acres and encompassed the springs and town. All the town buildings that had been established on the east side of the river can be seen, as the Army fort was on the west side of the river. In an attempt to gain ownership of the springs under the mineral laws of the United States, Byron Roberts & Co. filed a case against Henry Foote requesting Foote's Valentine Scrip filing be canceled. Examinations were conducted, and the mining claim was found to be non-mineral in character and a determination was made that lands containing mineral springs other than salt springs are not reserved from disposal as agricultural lands. (Courtesy of General Land Office Records.)

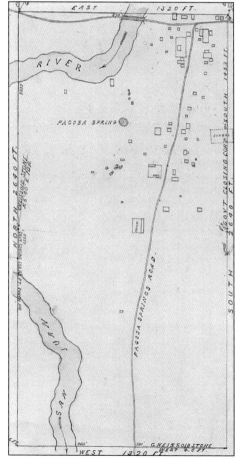

In the 1800s, thousands of workers like these constructed the early railroads throughout the country. These workers are building the Denver & Rio Grande (D&RG) Railroad through Archuleta County. The D&RG ran south from Denver to Pueblo, Colorado Springs, and Alamosa, where it turned west and bypassed Pagosa on its way to Durango and then Utah. The spread of logging and lumber mills following the arrival of the railroad created a number of communities across the county. (Courtesy of Deborah Archuleta.)

A man with a string of fish is pictured on the north side of the San Juan River; bathhouses, which were constructed by 1892, are in the background on the right (south) side of the river. The bathhouses (one for men and one for women) were constructed by the Pagosa Springs Company. James L. Byers, John Conover, and A.C. VanDyne formed the company to buy and manage the springs. (Courtesy of Fort Lewis College, Center of Southwest Studies.)

This photograph, taken after 1897, shows the hot springs. The white church steeple belonged to Pagosa's first church, the First Episcopal Methodist Church, which was built in 1897. Two people can be seen sitting on a bench looking out on the spring. From 1883 to 1910, the Pagosa Springs Company owned the hot springs and the bathhouses. Hot water was piped from the spring to the bathhouses, where men and women could separately soak in the mineral waters. (Courtesy of the La Plata County Historical Society.)

The Grand Army of the Republic Post No. 104, the Gen. Ed Hatcher Post, was formed in the late 1800s in Pagosa Springs. The Grand Army of the Republic was a fraternal organization of Union Civil War veterans. From left to right are Sanford Cotton, Abner Thompson, John Wingate, Elliot Halstead, Ephreham K. (E.K.) Caldwell, John Dowell, Jim Weber, Henry Fowler, Nathaniel L. Hayden, Tom McMullen, Eudolphus M. (E.M.) Taylor, J.W. Boles, McK. DeMotte, John Sparks, and W.L. Hyler. (Courtesy of Pagosa Springs American Legion Post No. 108.)

A locomotive crew, likely working on getting the rail line up and running, are sitting outside eating lunch in front of the engine around 1899. In that year, Alexander T. (A.T.) Sullenberger contracted with the Denver & Rio Grande to develop the Rio Grande & Pagosa Northern Railroad. With its completion in 1900, it connected Pagosa Springs south to Pagosa Junction, and therefore the wider world, on the Denver & Rio Grande Railroad. (Courtesy of Fort Lewis College, Center of Southwest Studies.)

This was one of the early boardinghouses in Pagosa. By 1900, there were seven hotels in town and half as many boardinghouses or homes where one could rent a room. (Courtesy of Franklin Anderson.)

This 1900s studio portrait shows one of Pagosa's early pioneer families, the Macht family. From left to right are (first row) siblings Harry, Emma, and Jule; (second row) Joe, William "Will," and their half brother Charles Betts. Widow Victoria Macht moved to Pagosa with her young sons Joe, Harry, Will, and daughter Emma in 1883. The family first lived in one of the buildings in town abandoned by the fort before moving to start a ranch out on Turkey Creek Road. (Courtesy of the R.D. Hott estate.)

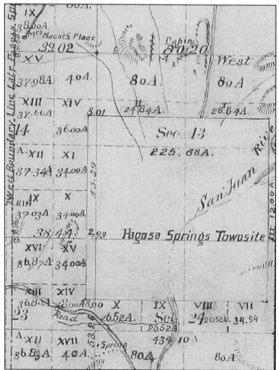

This is an 1888 plat map of the Pagosa Springs townsite. Of note is the location of Victoria Macht's place at upper left; it was the only family location noted by name on the whole map. (Courtesy of General Land Office Records.)

Two

1900s

Here is the 1900 Fourth of July parade in downtown Pagosa Springs. The Fourth of July was celebrated in Pagosa Springs since its inception, starting when the original Fort Lewis was here. It is interesting to speculate on the story behind this photograph. In 1900, there were no local families with the surname Kurtz, but there was one well-known photographer in the country by the name of Kurtz who had a studio in New York City—did he possibly venture West on a trip? (Author's collection.)

This photograph, featuring the natural hot springs in the foreground, was taken in the early 1900s, as Archuleta Mercantile has now been constructed downtown. Business signs visible in the background include those for Commercial Hotel and Oompaul. An oompaul is a very distinctive pipe, and this business appears to be Pagosa's first smoke/pipe shop. (Courtesy of the La Plata County Historical Society.)

Sheep are being sheared on José Marcelino (J.M.) Archuleta Jr.'s ranch in Edith. The Archuletas ran a couple thousand head of sheep in those days. In the early 1900s, J.M. established Archuleta Mercantile downtown in the location where the Liberty Theatre is now. (Courtesy of Franklin Anderson.)

Pictured are voter registrations for Precinct No. 4 in Archuleta County in October 1903. All the voters listed Trujillo as their place of residence; they represent many of the Hispanic families that resided in southern Archuleta County, with Archuleta, Garcia, Gallegos, Lucero, Silva, Trujillo, Martinez, and Quintana being the most dominant surnames on the roll. Below is the A page, showing the Archuleta, Aguilar, and Atincio entries. (Both, courtesy of Deborah Archuleta.)

STATE OF COLORADO, ss. October 13 1903
COUNTY OF Archuleta

I, J. a. Latta, do solemnly swear, in the presence of the ever living God, that I will honestly and faithfully discharge the duties of Registrar of Registration District 4, in Election Precinct No. 4 in the County of Archuleta and State aforesaid, according to law, and to the best of my skill and ability.

Subscribed and sworn to before me this Tuesday 13 day of October A. D. 1903.
J. a. Latta
Luis Lucero
Judge of Registry

STATE OF COLORADO, ss. Ja Oct. 27 1903
COUNTY OF Archuleta

I, J. a. Latta, do solemnly swear, in the presence of the ever living God, that I will honestly and faithfully discharge the duties of Registrar of Registration District, in Election Precinct No. 4 in the County of Archuleta and State aforesaid, according to law, and to the best of my skill and ability.

Subscribed and sworn to before me this Oct 27 day of Tuesday. A. D. 1903.
J. a. Latta
D. D. Archuleta
Judge of Registry

STATE OF COLORADO, ss. November 2nd 1903
COUNTY OF Archuleta

I, Ja Latta, do solemnly swear, in the presence of the ever living God, that I will honestly and faithfully discharge the duties of Registrar of Registration District four, in Election Precinct No. 4 in the County of Archuleta and State aforesaid, according to law, and to the best of my skill and ability.

Subscribed and sworn to before me this Second day of November A. D. 1903.
Joseph A Latta
Luis Lucero
Judge of Registry

NAMES OF ELECTORS

J. D. Archuleta
Mrs .. Archuleta
.. A. D. Archuleta
.. Demetrio Archuleta
.. Mrs Archuleta
.. Candido Archuleta
Mrs A. D. Archuleta

Archuleta. Vidal
Salaman. Aguilar
Mrs . Aguilar
Donaciano Archuleta
Mrs Archuleta
Alcario. Archuleta
Alcario. Atincio
Mrs .. Atincio
Jose Atincio
Mrs Atincio

This 1901 photograph, taken by early Pagosa resident and photographer Gordon O'Neal, shows a Rio Grande & Pagosa Northern train at the Pagosa Springs station. Pagosa could only be reached by stagecoach until train service began on the momentous day of October 22, 1900. The Rio Grande & Pagosa Northern Railroad simplified transportation of freight, livestock, people, and mail, and Pagosa Springs prospered with this new connection to the outside world. (Courtesy of the La Plata County Historical Society.)

Harry Lattin and Marion Hotz are pictured at the Biggs Mill logging operations in the Edith area around 1907. John and Samuel Biggs operated a large lumber operation near Chama in the late 1800s. In 1895, the Biggs Lumber Company put a mill in at Chromo, the first large mill in Archuleta County. Also in 1895, E.M. Biggs and the New Mexico Lumber Company put in a mill at Edith where the timber was transported out of the region by connection to the Denver & Rio Grande in Lumberton. The Biggses were major competitors to Sullenberger's operations prior to his making the railroad connection to Pagosa Springs and dominating the local industry. (Courtesy of Franklin Anderson.)

This 1904 photograph features Sullenberger's Pagosa Lumber Company sawmill in Pagosa Junction where the company was originally based. The mill shown here predated the Pagosa Lumber Company mill that was built in 1905 and 1906 in Pagosa Springs. Before the railroad was built to Pagosa Springs and Sullenberger's head of operations moved north, Pagosa Junction rivaled Pagosa Springs in size. (Courtesy of the Western History Collection, Denver Public Library.)

Another Biggs logging operation is seen here. An engine is pulling logs over a railroad trestle bridge. Marion Hotz is sitting on top of the large logs being transported to the mill. (Courtesy of Franklin Anderson.)

This photograph shows the amount of effort it took to thresh grain; here, multiple farming families join together to help in the process. The farming and ranching lifestyle meant people

would be willing and wanting to help their neighbors out, which helped form strong communities. (Courtesy of the R.D. Hott estate.)

Here are interior views of an early 1900s ranch house. Above is the Mill Creek Ranch, north of town. China is on display in the breakfronts, and people sit around the stove in the corner of the room. This room was a gathering place, where women would sew and children would play games on the rugs. Both photographs feature members of the Macht family. (Both, courtesy of the R.D. Hott estate.)

Hay has been cut and is being put up for the winter with the assistance of the hay derrick. Ranch life certainly was not easy, and one had to prepare year-round to be able to have everything needed to make it through the winter. (Courtesy of the R.D. Hott estate.)

Here is an overview of the business portion of Pagosa Springs looking south. The photograph was taken between 1906 and 1907, since in the background smoke is rising from the Pagosa Lumber Company mill, which was built in 1905–1906, and the Methodist church, which burned down in December 1907, is visible in the foreground. (Courtesy of Community United Methodist Church.)

When every person in town did not own a camera, momentous events such as the birth of a baby or a marriage were documented with a studio portrait for those who could afford it. At left is John and Alice Johnson's formal wedding picture from 1903. The portrait of Lois Lucile Parr below at seven months old was taken in 1906 at Acme Art Gallery, Pagosa's pioneer photography studio. (Both, courtesy of the R.D. Hott estate.)

This Acme Art Gallery photograph shows the First Methodist Episcopal Church fire of December 17, 1907. It is labeled "Third Stage of Fire." The Methodist church caught fire and burned down just near the end of a big renovation project. (Courtesy of Community United Methodist Church.)

Pagosa's First Methodist Episcopal Church is seen here after the fire; Gordon O'Neal took this Acme Art Gallery photograph. Over the winter, money was raised, fire insurance funds were received, and in the summer of 1908, the church was rebuilt under the direction of Harry and Will Macht. The church was reconstructed in the same location with almost the same design, but an extra room was added onto the south side of the building. (Courtesy of Community United Methodist Church.)

A boy is standing in front of a house and barn on Lewis Street; this house still exists and is in use behind the current US Forest Service complex. In the days before automobiles, each family had a barn to keep their horses in. (Courtesy of the R.D. Hott estate.)

This picture of the First Baptist Church was taken from the 1911 Methodist church souvenir booklet. The First Baptist Church congregation was formed in 1896. They published a cookbook in 1902 with recipes adapted to high-altitude cooking to try to raise funds to pay for the construction of a church building, which was completed in 1903. The church lasted until the 1930s, and when the congregation was floundering, its membership was invited to join the First Methodist Episcopal Church. The building was torn down in 1939, and the Macht family built a home on its location. (Courtesy of Feather Your Nest.)

This 1909 photograph looking down Pagosa Street shows all the storefronts, many with false fronts, and the wooden sidewalks the town installed in 1900. The powerline and the arc light hanging over the intersection are also noticeable developments that came in the 1900s. The town replaced the gas streetlights that had been installed in 1895 with the carbon arc lamps shown here in 1902. Arc lamps were the first type of electric streetlights and were introduced into the United States in the 1880s. (Courtesy of the Western History Collection, Denver Public Library.)

An ox-drawn wagon is stopped in town on the corner of San Juan and Pagosa Streets around 1909. Facing north, the photograph shows the corner of the bank building with the sign that reads, "Citizens Bank of Pagosa Springs." Just past one of the bank signs is a banner advertising undertaking, evidence that the bank building was shared with Hatcher Hardware and George Hatcher, one of the three brother-owners, also ran a funeral service parlor out of the building. (Courtesy of Fort Lewis College, Center of Southwest Studies.)

Merchant David Lowenstein, seen here, was born in Bavaria and moved to America in 1860. In the 1890s, he owned a grocery store in Durango near the Strater, and then in 1900 moved to Pagosa and bought the store on the corner of Pagosa and Fourth Streets. He ran a men's clothing store there from 1900 until he died in 1921. In 1922, his daughter Hortense took it over with her new husband, Louis, and the name of the store was changed to Goodman's after her married name. (Courtesy of the Goodman family.)

In this overview of the town are homes, a hotel, and stables in the foreground. Steam is rising from the springs at left center, and right of that is a field of encrustation caused by the spring water. The bathhouses, the San Juan River, and Main Street all follow, and the school is on the hill in the background. In the back of the business district, a large barn with a distinctive roof is visible, which is the livery. Prior to automobiles, every town had a livery to stable the horses of travelers. (Courtesy of the La Plata County Historical Society.)

Three

1910s

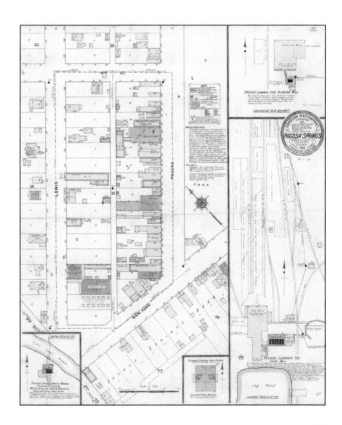

The 1910 Sanborn Fire Insurance Company map of Pagosa Springs lists the population at 900. Inset maps show the layout of the Pagosa Lumber Company's sawmill and planing mill. (Courtesy of the Library of Congress.)

This panoramic view of town in the 1910s shows how the town had expanded. The tracks of the Denver & Rio Grande Railroad, the train depot, and water tower are in the foreground. Noticeable in the middle ground are the school on the hill and the Arlington Hotel downtown. The 1911 business directory of Pagosa Springs shows that lumber/timber, real estate, saloons, and hotels/ boardinghouses were the most plentiful enterprises. Also listed were four churches: the Baptist, Catholic, Episcopal, and Methodist Episcopal. (Courtesy of the Western History Collection, Denver Public Library.)

State representative J.B. "Brice" Patterson and grandson Harry "Bud" Patterson, Pagosa residents, are seen here during the time that Brice Patterson was serving his second term representing Archuleta, Mineral, and Hinsdale Counties. After moving to Pagosa from Silverton in 1909, Patterson bought several ranches in the area and the Arlington Hotel and served as the town mayor prior to serving in the House of Representatives. (Courtesy of Dean Cox.)

This Arlington Hotel & Bath House advertisement was taken from a 1910 First Methodist Episcopal Church souvenir booklet. As listed in Pagosa's 1911 business directory, "J.B. Patterson & Son" were the managers. The Arlington consisted of a hotel building, bathhouse, and 15 tents that would later be improved into cabins. (Courtesy of Feather Your Nest.)

Arlington Hotel & Bath House

Pagosa Springs, Colorado.

RATES, $1.50 TO $2.50 PER DAY.

Heated by Natural Hot Water. The Arlington has the best Bath accommodations in the southwest; separate pools for ladies and gentlemen; those who are afflicted with stomach trouble or rheumatism, kidney or blood diseases will find that these waters will afford a speedy, permanent cure. Those who desire to take a trip to the mountains for big game will do well to stop with us —we have a fine pack of bear and lion dogs and can find big game

J. B. PATTERSON & SON, Proprietors

House tents in connection with the hotel for those who desire them.

This photograph from the Macht family collection shows Jule and Belle's daughter Fern Macht with her classmates outside of the town's school, now referred to as the old school on the hill. (Courtesy of the R.D. Hott estate.)

The inside of the school is decorated for the Christmas holiday. In front of the desks, two trees are decorated for Christmas, and even some stocking are hung by the fireplace. (Courtesy of the R.D. Hott estate.)

This 1915 photograph shows schoolchildren, from left to right, (first row) Jullian Martinez, unidentified, Everett Dunagan, Ray Rank, Wilma Morgan, unidentified, Smith, Bonnie Railey, Milford Johnson, Ellis Speelman, and unidentified; (second row) unidentified, Elva Parr, and unidentified; (third row) two unidentified, Fern Macht, Edna Kleckuer, and two unidentified; (fourth row) Isaac Martinez, two unidentified, Clark Speelman, Hilda Keith, Irene Speelman, Mary Spickard, unidentified, Anna Mae Goodman, Helen Bryant, and Lucy Flaugh; (fifth row) Marvin Arnold (holding onto the pillar), teacher Maud Bayles, two unidentified, Ted Lattin, and three unidentified. (Courtesy of the R.D. Hott estate.)

This view of the main business district in approximately 1910 was taken from across the San Juan River. Business signs visible include Hatcher Mercantile Co.; Happyland Theatre; G.S. Jones, Dry Goods & Groceries; Groceries, Hay & Grain; General Merchandise; and W.H. Norton. Several men stand around a fancy barbershop pole on the wooden boardwalk that lines the street. (Courtesy of the Western History Collection, Denver Public Library.)

This postcard features the Pagosa Lumber Company Mill in the early 1910s. The white house at center is A.T. Sullenberger's home, which is still standing today. The current high school is where the lumber mill used to be. (Author's collection.)

Pagosa Springs Sun

A Live Wire Newspaper,

$2.00 Per Year. $100 for Six Mos.

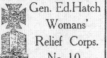 Gen. Ed.Hatch
Womans'
Relief Corps.
No. 10.

Mrs. C. D. CALDWELL,
President.

Mrs. MAUDE DAY,
Secretary.

Meets Every First and Third
Thursday at 3 o'olock
P. M.

W. W. Mullins

Tonsorial
Parlor

Only First Class Workmen
Employed. Call and see
us for anything in the
barber line.

Pagosa Springs, Colo

Pagosa Springs New Era

Oldest Paper in Archuleta County.

Subscription Price $2.00 per year.

C. A. DAY, Editor and Manager.

Seen here are advertisements for the *Pagosa Springs Sun* and the *Pagosa Springs New Era*, among others, in the 1910 Methodist church souvenir booklet. The 1911 business directory lists two newspapers operating in town: the New Era Publishing Company's *Pagosa Springs New Era*, with editor C.A. Day and secretary-manager E.K. Caldwell, and the Pagosa Publishing Company's *Pagosa Springs Sun*, with publisher-secretary W.E. Furrow. (Courtesy of Feather Your Nest.)

In 1916, a man is snaking logs west of the town of Pagosa Springs. This location is now considered to be in town; as of 2020, it is the location of the Wyndham Pagosa Resort. Snaking logs involved pulling cut logs with livestock to where they could be loaded onto a train. (Courtesy of Ray's Hair Care.)

James "Jim" Carlin's cattle team is seen here at Sunetha Flats, four miles west of the historic downtown area of Pagosa. Fourteen bulls are pulling a load of lumber while two men pose alongside the team. Sunetha was formed as a stop on the train when Sullenberger extended the line to Pagosa for his lumber industry. According to the San Juan Historical Society's *Remembrances*, the name was made up, borrowing "su" from the first part of Sullenberger's name, "net" from Newton, and "ha" from Hatcher. (Courtesy of Fort Lewis College, Center of Southwest Studies.)

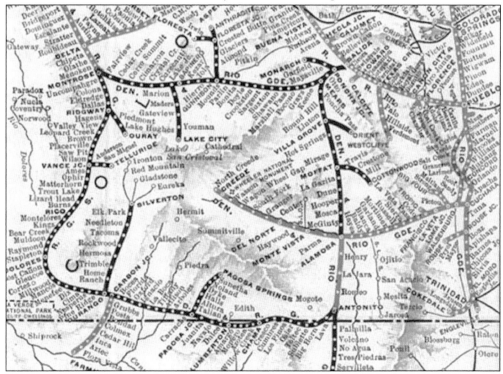

This is a close-up of the local area from a map of the Denver & Rio Grande Railroad system in 1900. (Courtesy of Wikimedia.)

Denver & Rio Grande engine No. 65, the *San Cristoval*, is pictured near Pagosa Springs in the 1910s. The locomotive was an 1880 Baldwin-manufactured 56 Class with 2-8-0 wheel arrangement. It was leased to the Silverton Railroad in 1890 and rebuilt as an 0-8-0 in 1908. It ended its career and was scrapped in 1917. (Author's collection.)

Early roads in this region were obstacles themselves. Here, a car is broken down on the side of the road near Pagosa. In February 1899, some of the first automobiles in Colorado were displayed in Denver. Though they had to be shipped from factories on the East Coast or built by hand, vehicles spread throughout the state. By 1902, there was pressure to improve the existing system of wagon roads in the state to handle the automobiles. On September 9, 1912, there were enough automobiles in the local area that a town ordinance was adopted to regulate their use in Pagosa. (Courtesy of Fort Lewis College, Center of Southwest Studies.)

A house and the town park gazebo are seen in the water of the San Juan River that has overflowed its banks in the historic flood of 1911. Drenched with constant rain, on October 5 and 6, rivers flooded, and every town located near a river in Southwestern Colorado suffered massive flooding, the worst yet to this day. The flood took out every bridge in the county and the telegraph and telephone lines, destroyed Pagosa's waterworks and electrical plant, and ruined the railroad tracks, which stopped train service and mail delivery. (Courtesy of Fort Lewis College, Center of Southwest Studies.)

Photographed after the 1911 flood wiped out the bridge over the San Juan River and before the new bridge was built in 1912, a tractor is hauling lumber near the junction of San Juan and Pagosa Streets. In the background, a wooden barricade marks the end of the road. (Courtesy of Fort Lewis College, Center of Southwest Studies.)

St. Francis congregation is seen at the ruins of their church that burned down in 1915. From left to right are Margarita Maria Quintana, Maria Genoveva Silva, Rosalia Martinez, Dolorita "Lola" Garcia, Maria Magdalena Martinez, Sarita Garcia, Julianita Quintana, Luis Marcelino Quintana, Maria Inez Martinez, Antonio Jose Martinez, Maria Isabel "Isabelita" Gallegos, Maria Elviria Candelaria, Carlota Martinez, Barbarita Rivas, Tomas Valdez, Maria Perfilia Valdez, Maria Jesus, Juliana, Crusita Tafoya, Alfonso or Ismel Tafoya, Rev. Anthony Segrara, Ninfa Gallegos, Juan Gallegos, Rosa Candelaria, Celestino Garcia, Roman Gurule, Facundo Quintana, Jose Margarito

Martinez, Benigno Martinez, Maria Trinidad Martinez, Jose Teofilo Martinez, Victoriana Martinez, Alcario Gallegos, Carolina Martinez, Francisco Gallegos, Veronise Sisneros, Anacleto Sisneros, Ferminia O'Cana, Rubio Gallegos, Benito Gallegos, Manuel Gurule, Roberto "Luberto" Gurule, Jose Antonio Tafoya, Francisco Martinez, Theodorita Martinez, Lino Garcia, Sarita Chavez, Daniel Gallegos, Refugio Gallegos, Desiderio Chavez, Victoriana Gurule, and Guillermo Quintana. (Courtesy of the Gallegos family.)

This postcard of Upper Fourmile Lake was mailed out of Pagosa Junction in 1912. Upper Fourmile Lake is a subalpine lake now in the Weminuche Wilderness, 17 miles north of Pagosa Springs. The Weminuche Wilderness is the largest wilderness area in Colorado at 499,771 acres. It was designated a wilderness by Congress in 1975 and is managed by the San Juan National Forest. (Author's collection.)

"Dutch" Henry Born left his famous horse thief and outlaw past when he settled in this area. Pictured here is Born's Lake, where Born and his family had a homestead and started a tourist resort focused on trout fishing. The lake was described in a 1910 Pagosa souvenir guide as "the sportman's paradise; the pleasure lover's retreat; and the delight of the infirm and weak." (Courtesy of the R.D. Hott estate.)

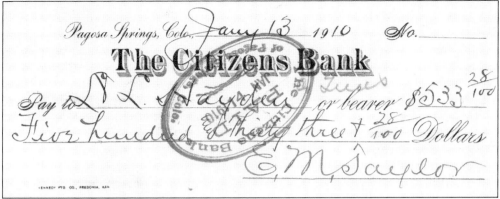

This 1910 Citizens Bank personal check was made out for $533.28 and paid by Archuleta County's first treasurer, Eudolphus M. (E.M.) Taylor. This check could either be from Taylor's loan business (one of his many ventures) or for something he purchased, which would have been considered a large expense in this fairly remote area in 1910. That amount would be about $14,000 in 2020. (Author's collection.)

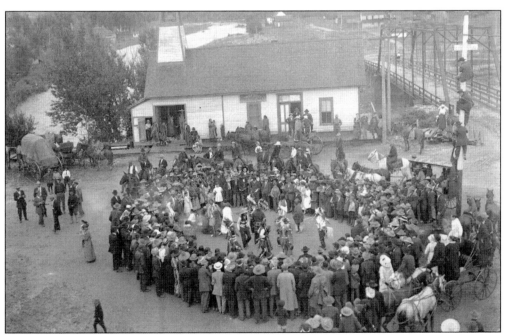

A group of Ute performers is seen dancing outside of town hall and drawing quite the crowd. These groups would be invited to perform, and while they were not paid for their performance, they did take any money the crowd gave them. The date is unknown, but the bridge in the photograph was built in 1912. (Courtesy of Fort Lewis College, Center of Southwest Studies.)

In 1913, the Colorado State Highway Commission was looking for a highway route over the San Juan Mountains. Wolf Creek was chosen over the old wagon route through Elwood Pass due to its steep grade. The new route was surveyed by E. Malony, engineer for the Colorado State Highway Commission, and state highway engineer Mark U. Waltrous; the survey party is seen here. (Courtesy of Colorado Department of Transportation.)

L.J. Chapman's crew is building the original Wolf Creek Pass road in 1915. Crew members are on the cliffs on the left dynamiting rock. Writing on the picture reads, "Sean after shot was fired by Chapman's crew" and points out a rock that was just dislodged that measured 10 feet square and 35 feet long. When it was completed, it was the highest automobile road pass in the state at 10,850 feet. (Courtesy of Colorado Department of Transportation.)

A line of cars is driving through downtown Pagosa. This photograph is said to have been taken the day that Wolf Creek Pass opened in 1916. The opening of the pass ushered in another wave of Pagosa history as the town was accessible from cities to the east. Although it was initially only open during the summer months, the new highway offered a great opportunity for encouraging tourism and obtaining goods. The opening ceremonies were held on August 21, 1916. (Courtesy of Fort Lewis College, Center of Southwest Studies.)

Cars are stopped on the road to Wolf Creek Pass. The men are helping reopen the road on the Pagosa side after a snowfall had closed it. Although Wolf Creek Pass opened in 1916, it was not open year-round for another 20 years, until 1936. Mountainous areas in Colorado posed extreme difficulties for keeping roads snow-free, and many times, the only option was for locals to join the highway department in the effort to shovel out snowdrifts. (Courtesy of Fort Lewis College, Center of Southwest Studies.)

This is a view of the Pagosa Lumber Company sawmill in 1915. Writing on the picture reads, "Pagosa Lumber Company Plainer and Sawmill." The mill consists of several buildings situated around railroad tracks. Stacks of lumber have been placed next to the tracks, ready for transport. (Courtesy of the Western History Collection, Denver Public Library.)

In this typical serious-looking family portrait are Malinda and Rudy Flaugh and their children Lloyd and Emma. Malinda and Rudy were early homesteaders who came to Pagosa as newlyweds in 1888. Portraits at this time were likely the only photograph someone would have, so an effort was made to look as elegant and serious as possible, following painting customs. (Courtesy of the R.D. Hott estate.)

Two women on horseback are seen in their winter riding clothes; Hortense Goodman is on the left. Hortense grew up in Pagosa, the daughter of David and Fanny Lowenstein. She met her future husband, Louis Goodman, in St. Louis where she was staying with family, and he followed her back to Pagosa and helped her to take over the family business after they married. Hortense was a tough lady, who, according to Goodman family history, was the first woman to drive over Wolf Creek Pass. (Courtesy of the Goodman family.)

On March 12, 1919, fire destroyed five Pagosa Street buildings, including A.T. Sullenberger's hotel, the telephone building, and the millinery store. In the foreground, Pagosa's pioneer dentist Bert "Doc" Ellsworth is seen to the left of the woman in the light-colored hat. Doc Ellsworth had moved to Pagosa in 1911 and had a dental practice next door to Lowenstein's Gent's Furnishings, which was later renamed Goodman's Department Store. After the fire, Sullenberger immediately began rebuilding the hotel. (Courtesy of the La Plata County Historical Society.)

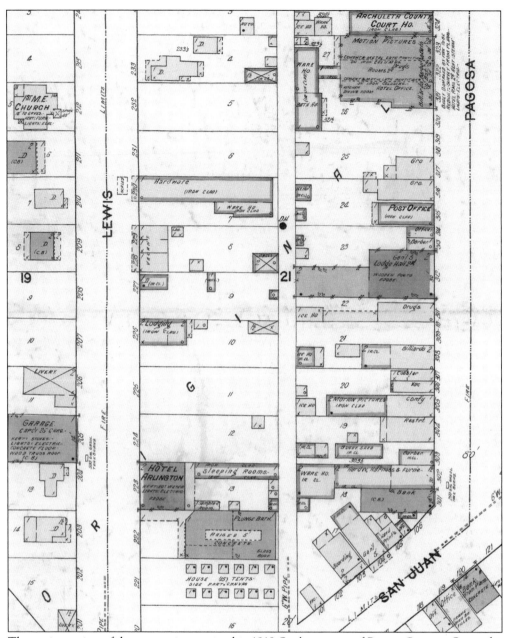

The main section of downtown is seen in this 1919 Sanborn map of Pagosa Springs. Since the 1917 closing of the Pagosa Lumber Company mill and headquarters removed the largest employer in town, the population listed on this map had gone down to 700. (Courtesy of the Library of Congress.)

Four

1920s

Everyone is getting ready to eat at a picnic in the Blanco Basin on July 4, 1925. US Forest Service ranger Harry L. Norris, stationed at the Square Top Ranger Station from 1919 through 1925, took the photograph. (Courtesy of the San Juan National Forest.)

Pictured in 1924 are the Pagosa Springs natural hot springs (foreground) and downtown buildings (background). Less downtown businesses have wooden false fronts now that the town passed an ordinance in 1921, after several destructive fires, requiring exterior walls be constructed of either brick, stone, or concrete. (Courtesy of the Western History Collection, Denver Public Library.)

Pagosa's school on the hill was engulfed in flames on January 23, 1924. (Courtesy of Fort Lewis College, Center of Southwest Studies.)

High school sophomores Aubery Thomas, Rossa McKinley, Marguerite Cato, and Julia "Juju" Patterson are posing at the edge of the hot springs in 1925. The group was going to school in the Methodist church until the new school could be constructed. They ended up being in the first class to graduate from the new school. (Courtesy of Dean Cox.)

This 1925 photograph is labeled, "Citizens Bank—the only one in the world heated by natural water." In 1909, Citizens Bank, which had been formed in 1908, moved into to this location, sharing a building with Hatcher Hardware. Hatcher Hardware was operated by brothers George, James, and Elmer Hatcher. The two-story brick building caught fire several times; following the devastating 1943 fire, a completely new building was constructed. (Courtesy of the Western History Collection, Denver Public Library.)

A Hersch Mercantile Co. aluminum trade token is seen here; the other side reads, "Good for 10¢ in Merchandise." The height of trade, or barter, tokens' popularity was from the 1870s to the 1920s. This token likely dates to the early 1920s after Hatcher Mercantile changed ownership and the name was changed to Hersch Mercantile. (Author's collection.)

This Denver & Rio Grande Western engine No. 271 was a Baldwin-built 2-8-0 narrow-gauge locomotive. This photograph was taken in 1923 in Pagosa Springs by Otto Perry. At this time, the line was no longer used for logging but stayed in operation for passenger and freight traffic. Otto Perry was a well-known railroad photographer who rode the rails around the country, documenting railroad history in still and moving pictures. (Courtesy of the Western History Collection, Denver Public Library.)

This photograph, taken by photographer George L. Beam, was labeled, "Mirror Lake, outside Pagosa Springs." Beam was the company photographer for the Denver & Rio Grande Railroad. His photographs include an extensive collection of railroad trains and tracks, but he also documented scenic vistas of the areas that tourists might visit while using the railroad. (Courtesy of the Western History Collection, Denver Public Library.)

In this 1928 photograph, Thelma Hauser and Julia "Juju" Patterson are posing with the rabbits they shot and strung up. Thelma married Earl Mullins in 1928, and Juju married John "Lee" Cox in 1929. (Courtesy of Dean Cox.)

The Blue Mountain lookout tower was built in the 1920s and was one of the first lookout towers constructed in the San Juan National Forest, which was created by Theodore Roosevelt in 1905. This location was only used as a lookout for a short time, and not many photographs of it exist. (Courtesy of the R.D. Hott estate.)

MOTHER NATURE HEATS THIS SCHOOL
The new school building at Pagosa Springs, Colo., heated by natural hot water and completed at a cost of $75,000.

This November 1, 1925, picture shows off Pagosa's new schoolhouse in the Denver *Rocky Mountain News*. The building was designed to be heated by the hot springs and replaced the school on the hill that burned down in 1924. School started in this building in September 1925. (Courtesy of Archuleta School District.)

The new Archuleta County Courthouse, designed by Denver architect Eugene Groves, was constructed in 1928 and is still used today. Like several other buildings in town, the courthouse was also designed to be heated by the natural hot springs. (Author's collection.)

Howard Anderson, with his rifle and the black bear he shot, is pictured outside his family's home in Chromo, located at the southern extent of what local historian John Motter calls "Pagosa Country." The *Pagosa Springs Sun* featured the columns "Juanita Items" and "Chromo Items," which kept those in town apprised of what was going on in the rest of Archuleta County. Below is a 1927 "Chromo Items." (Left, courtesy of Franklin Anderson; below, courtesy of Feather Your Nest.)

CHROMO ITEMS

R. L .Ewell is in Dulce again. Can't keep Bob away from his Apache friends.

The snow is about gone and the roads too—at least the passable part of them.

Some of the ranchmen are putting up ice while others are waiting for colder weather.

Mr. Shahan is quite sick. Dr. Denham of Chama was called to see him Wednesday night.

Ike Russell has bought property in Monte Vista, but will still keep his present business here.

All the measles patients have recovered and no further spread of the disease is anticipated.

The Largo brothers were up from the reservation buying horses from Horace Brooks and Mr. Graham.

Bob and Francis Shahan came home for the Christmas vacation. They went back to school Monday.

Bob Henry came home from the valley a few days ago. Reports his cattle in fine condition and wintering nicely.

Three lovely ladies are posing for a photograph in the 1920s; Jennie "Belle" Macht is at center. The photograph was taken at the family ranch near Square Top Mountain. (Courtesy of the R.D. Hott estate.)

Jennie "Belle" Macht is driving either a 1926 or 1927 Ford Model T Tudor. The Tudor was a two-door sedan model with two rows of seats and an enclosed body and fixed top. After 1927, Ford discontinued the Model T and switched to producing the Model A. (Courtesy of the R.D. Hott estate.)

61

Here, brothers Rex and Emmett Hott are fooling around outside the family's home on Spring Creek. This house was the second in the county to get running water. (Courtesy of the R.D. Hott estate.)

Emmett Hott, pictured at the Spring Creek Ranch near Tiffany, is doing his trick roping. (Courtesy of the R.D. Hott estate.)

Five

1930s

This 1933 photograph is an example of the type of check dam construction that was built across Archuleta County during the 1930s. The dams were built to help reverse the erosion that had started from livestock grazing. During the Great Depression, Pagosa's population declined as there was no industry in the area to employee people. However, work on the national forests expanded exponentially as the US Forest Service role began changing and federal relief programs conducted land improvement projects across the country. In the 1930s, crews making improvements in the San Juan National Forest included the following New Deal programs and agencies: Civilian Conservation Corps (CCC), Work Projects Administration (WPA), Emergency Relief Act (ERA), Emergency Conservation Work (ECW) Act, and the National Industrial Recovery Act (NRA). (Courtesy of the San Juan National Forest.)

Two Model Ts meet in front of the Sturdivant House on San Juan Street. William "Billy" Kern and his wife, Elizabeth "Liz," had this house built for them in 1890. Liz ran the town's post office and stationery store out of it, and Billy had the US mail contract that covered the area between Summitville and Pagosa Springs. Other roles Billy held over the years in Pagosa were stagecoach driver and sheriff. Later, Frank Sturdivant and family lived in the house for a long time, hence the name. This house is still standing today. (Courtesy of Dean Cox.)

At first glance, this looks like Dr. Mary Winter Fisher's beloved pet bear, Pickles. However, this photograph was taken in Pagosa in 1932, after her death. This could be Pickles in the care of another owner, or it could be an entirely different pet bear. (Courtesy of Dean Cox.)

Pictured inside the train station in Pagosa, Ernest Smith is standing behind the ticket counter. This 1930s photograph was taken sometime prior to rail service to Pagosa ceasing in 1936. Smith was the last surviving charter member of Pagosa Springs American Legion Post No. 108 when he passed away in 1991. He had been a musician when he served in the Navy. Along with working at the train station, he also worked as a banker, city clerk, and county assessor. (Courtesy of Fort Lewis College, Center of Southwest Studies.)

Unidentified people are walking down the old steel bridge on San Juan Street. Visible in the background is the former shared town hall, library, and firehouse building. This bridge, built in 1912, was there until 1957 when a drunk driver hit it, causing it to crash into the river. (Courtesy of Dean Cox.)

Above is the outside of Goodman's Department Store, with its older wood facade. Pictured below around 1930, owners Hortense (center) and Louis Goodman (right) are working with a customer in the store. When Hortense's father owned the store, it sold only men's clothing, and when she and Louis took it over in 1922, they started selling women's clothes as well. (Both, courtesy of the Goodman family.)

Posing outside of Goodman's Department Store above is owner Louis Goodman. The family has a picture of each subsequent generation recreating this photograph. The current owner, Hayley Goodman, is the fifth generation to run the store. The store is the longest single family–owned and –operated business in Pagosa. Below is a view from inside the store. Both photographs were taken in the late 1930s. (Both, courtesy of the Goodman family.)

This Sanborn real-photo postcard featuring Chimney Rock is labeled "W2162" in the right corner and is possibly from the 1930s. The W stands for Western Colorado, and the 2162 is the numerical order for that category. In the 1920s, Harold Sanborn started the Sanborn Souvenir Company in Denver. He took photographs of Colorado and Wyoming and made them into postcards for decades. (Author's collection.)

In Sanborn postcard W-1784, the beauty of the snow cover on Pagosa Peak towering over town can be seen. The Pagosa Springs school building, constructed in 1925, is visible at center. The building originally served all grades but has since been used for different grade ranges, most often as a middle school. (Author's collection.)

This Sanborn postcard, W-1251, features the waterfall at Born's Lake. Its W-1251 designation means that it is older than the school photograph and Chimney Rock photograph on the previous page. All Sanborn postcards can be relatively dated this way. (Author's collection.)

Here is signage at the Born's Lake trailhead up the West Fork of the San Juan. Other than Born's Lake Resort and US Forest Service campgrounds, there are advertisements for tourist amenities at the Bruce Spruce Ranch, which is still there, and the Flying W Ranch, which no longer exists. (Courtesy of the San Juan National Forest.)

R.C. Meager was the superintendent of CCC Camp F-29-C. Camp F-29-C, named the Blanco Camp, was located outside Pagosa Springs, two miles up the Blanco River from Highway 17. Construction began on the camp in June 1933 and was completed in August. In later years, camp enrollees worked on improving the camp as it had been built fast as temporary structures. (Courtesy of the San Juan National Forest.)

At the time of this 1933 photograph, local Harry "Bud" Patterson was enrolled at Camp F-29-C. He was later sent to camps farther away from home. In this camp's early years, it was mostly populated with local men, and increasingly by those from out of state as the years went on. Over 35,000 men from Colorado were enrolled in the CCC, and more than 57,000 men from around the country served in the state. (Courtesy of Dean Cox.)

R.C. Meager took this picture of a roadside curve warning sign, located between town and the camp. Enacted by Pres. Franklin D. Roosevelt in 1933, the CCC was a New Deal program aimed at reducing unemployment among young men by giving them steady work improving the nation's landscape, public lands, and infrastructure. The majority of CCC camps in Colorado, including the Pagosa Springs camp (Camp F-29-C), were on US Forest Service lands. (Courtesy of the San Juan National Forest.)

Firefighting, forest restoration, and soil erosion control projects were the main sources of work for CCC crews in Colorado. Additionally, roads, trails, structures, and campgrounds were built in national forests and in state and national parks, like Mesa Verde. Existing irrigation infrastructure was repaired, and new ditches and canal systems were constructed statewide at Bureau of Reclamation camps. Here, Blanco Camp men are busy constructing the bridge over Trail Creek. (Courtesy of the San Juan National Forest.)

N.B. Apgar took this c. 1930 photograph of sheep being counted at the Turkey Springs counting pens. The sheep had to be counted when they were put on and taken off each range. A US Forest Service representative had to be there during the counting, and both the sheep herder and the forest service employee would count each sheep as it filed past them to ensure the correct numbers were tallied. (Courtesy of the San Juan National Forest.)

Pictured in 1935 is the guard station at Turkey Springs. A prior station had been built here in 1921, but when ranger John C. Baird and new his wife, Sally, were staying in it on their working honeymoon in 1929, they burned the station down while cooking their first breakfast together. This building was constructed by Baird in 1930 to replace the original. (Courtesy of the San Juan National Forest.)

In 1936, roads were finally able to open during the winter on Wolf Creek Pass. This scene from February 1936 shows a Caterpillar-mounted snowplow clearing snow on the summit of Wolf Creek Pass. (Courtesy of Colorado Department of Transportation.)

Another February 1936 scene shows the serious amount of snow that had to be cleared in the wintertime on Wolf Creek Pass. (Courtesy of Colorado Department of Transportation.)

A lot of road maintenance work was required to keep dirt roads in driving condition. Here on Wolf Creek Pass, a crawler tractor and a pull-behind grader are smoothing the road out. This crawler is a diesel-powered McCormick-Deering TracTracTor made by International Harvester. (Courtesy of Colorado Department of Transportation.)

This photograph, taken in town on Main Street at the corner of Lewis Street and orientated toward O'Neil Hill, shows a Ford Model A that had to be towed into town from Highway 160 after an accident that ended in a guardrail punching through the car. (Courtesy of Colorado Department of Transportation.)

Pictured is the Piedra Guard Station on the Upper Piedra. The guard station was built in the 1930s, which was when most of the development of the national forest happened in this region. This building still exists but not in its original location; it was sold to a private owner and moved. (Courtesy of the San Juan National Forest.)

Pictured are Lloyd Anderson and his kids on a horse in front of the road and gate of the Piedra Guard Station. Anderson, a government trapper working for the US Fish and Wildlife Service from 1936 to 1977, kept his horses there. (Courtesy of Franklin Anderson.)

Lloyd Anderson is pictured on horseback outside his family's home on Seventh Street. He was based out of Pagosa Springs, but the enormous territory he covered as a trapper went from near Chama, New Mexico, all the way to the old Fort Lewis by Hesperus. (Courtesy of Franklin Anderson.)

Here is an example of how much snow Pagosa used to get in town in the wintertime. Again, Lloyd Anderson is pictured on the same horse outside of the same house. Anderson lived in this house from 1933 until he passed away in 1982. (Courtesy of Franklin Anderson.)

Coyotes were the enemy of settlers, especially farmers and ranchers. The government hired trappers to help the sheep and cattle ranchers protect their livestock from coyotes, wolves, mountain lions, and bears. A big part of Lloyd Anderson's job was killing coyotes; he would trap, shoot, or poison them. (Courtesy of Franklin Anderson.)

Franklin Anderson had a pet coyote as a boy, a unique opportunity brought about by his dad being a government trapper. Lloyd, took the pup out of a den and brought her home. They named her Peggy and kept her for a few years. When Peggy killed some chickens in town, they gave her away. (Courtesy of Franklin Anderson).

This rare 1940s photograph of a bobcat comes from Lloyd Anderson's collection. (Courtesy of Franklin Anderson.)

When they were not working, families found time to have fun with their friends and relatives. During the Depression, when families had little money to spend on entertainment, many around here enjoyed going fishing. This group is fishing on the Navajo River. (Courtesy of Franklin Anderson.)

Six

1940s

People stand around the perimeter of what was called at different times the "Great Hot Spring," the "Big Pagosa Spring," or the "Mother Spring" in 1942. The spring itself still looks undeveloped; however, a pumphouse was built near it to provide water for the town's geothermal heating system. The spring is listed in the Colorado State Register of Historic Places as "the Great Pagosa Hot Spring." It is documented as a cultural site significant as a healing bath associated with an important event—the settlement of the region. (Courtesy of the Western History Collection, Denver Public Library.)

From left to right, Susie and John Cox and their daughter-in-law Julia "Juju" Cox watch grandchildren Alva Lee Cox and Dean Cox ride a mule. The square white cabins at right are part of the Arlington Hotel, which Juju managed. (Courtesy of Dean Cox.)

This photograph shows one of the necessary uses of time in the winter in this part of the country—shoveling snow! (Courtesy of the Harman estate.)

On the left is the Pagosa Springs Rangers Residence No. 1, which was built by ERA labor in 1937. It was built to house one of the two Forest Service rangers living in Pagosa. Both the rangers for the Pagosa and the Piedra ranger districts were stationed in Pagosa. Built in a unique (to this area) Mediterranean style, the building has been modified over the years, causing it to lose some of its character. For example, the impractical Spanish tile roof has been replaced with a metal roof. (Courtesy of the San Juan National Forest.)

In 1938, this building, the Pagosa Springs Rangers Residence No. 2, was erected for Forest Service ranger housing. Seen here in 1940, it was constructed in Pueblo style with a flat roof, structural brick walls covered with stucco, lintels over the doors and windows, and log vigas protruding from the outside walls. The building still stands, but unfortunately, with its many alterations over the decades, including the addition of a gabled roof to be able to shed snow, it is unrecognizable as a Pueblo-style Forest Service administrative facility. (Courtesy of the San Juan National Forest.)

Here are Fred and Lola Harman's ranch house buildings at their Red Ryder Ranch. Both buildings look like they are still under construction, with log siding and roofing still being put on, and a group of folks have come out to visit the ranch. (Courtesy of the Harman estate.)

Visitors to the Harmans' ranch house are dancing to music. Starting at left, Dorothy Marco, Lola Harman, Peggy Richards, and Paul Richards are identified. Fred Harman was a well-known celebrity in the 1940s, and for many years, it was announced in the newspaper when he and Lola were in town as well as when they had big-city visitors coming to stay with them. They frequently hosted visitors, ranging from local friends to fans from across the country, at their ranch. (Courtesy of the Harman estate.)

This picturesque view of the "Entering San Juan National Forest" sign on the side of Highway 160, about four miles northeast of Pagosa, was taken by Jay Higgins in 1940. This sign is next to the Treasure Guard Station. (Courtesy of the San Juan National Forest.)

This 1941 photograph, taken by Jay Higgins, is of the CCC-constructed Treasure Guard Station. This guard station is characteristic of many of the Bungalow-style stations constructed across the forest in the late 1930s as the Forest Service expanded its administration role of the national forest both locally and nationwide. (Courtesy of the San Juan National Forest.)

Above, smoke is billowing out of the windows of the Hatcher Hardware and Citizens Bank building in the fire that started May 26, 1943. Below, flames are reaching up from the building. The fire started in the Moorehead Apartment Building, and within 20 minutes, it spread to the whole block. Hoses have been connected to fire hydrants as people attempt to put out the flames. A pump was also put in the river to pump water up for fire suppression. (Both, courtesy of Ray's Hair Care.)

This building had caught on fire before, but this time it was completely destroyed, and a new one had to be constructed from scratch afterward. Citizens Bank; G.A. Alley Hardware, Furniture and Implements; Pagosa Bar; Moorehead Apartment Building; Montroy Apartment Building; the original Jackish Drug; Manhattan Café; and the meeting place and the records of the Ancient Free and Accepted Masons Pagosa Lodge No. 114 and the Pioneer Chapter of the Eastern Star were all a complete loss. (Both, courtesy of Ray's Hair Care.)

As a teenager, Fred Harman III worked on the family's Red Ryder Ranch during haying season. Fred grew up in the Upper Blanco Basin, served in the Navy, and had a long career working for CBS in New York City before retiring and moving back to Pagosa Springs. He and his wife, Norma, opened the Fred Harman Art Museum in Pagosa in 1983. (Courtesy of the Harman estate.)

This unidentified man is posing with his elk antler trophy, which is ready to go on the wall! (Courtesy of the Harman estate.)

It is time to vaccinate the calves. Here, a calf is being put in a branding table to help control it during the process. A product of Staggs and Co. of Henrietta, Texas, the branding table is labeled the "Staggs Branding Table." (Courtesy of the Harman estate.)

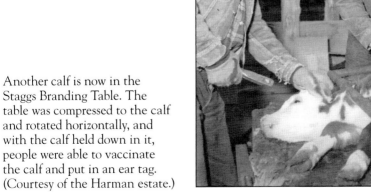

Another calf is now in the Staggs Branding Table. The table was compressed to the calf and rotated horizontally, and with the calf held down in it, people were able to vaccinate the calf and put in an ear tag. (Courtesy of the Harman estate.)

In this ranch scene, two cowboys are branding a horse on the left front shoulder. (Courtesy of the Harman estate.)

A squeeze chute, pictured, was a traditional way of getting a full-sized cow to hold still for needed work. (Courtesy of the Harman estate.)

This fun picture is the epitome of showing off for the camera! (Courtesy of the Harman estate.)

This picture shows it is not only boys who like to show off for the camera. (Courtesy of the Harman estate.)

It is branding time at the ranch. In this scene, two cowboys have each roped a leg, and one is even holding onto the tail, as they try to get the cow to the ground. (Courtesy of the Harman estate.)

As this cow lies immobilized on the ground, the brand is seared into its flesh, denoting its ownership. (Courtesy of the Harman estate.)

Here, a group is taking a break from helping out with the cows and having refreshments. The older man in the overalls is holding a syringe, indicating his role is likely giving vaccinations. (Courtesy of the Harman estate.)

Cousins Beverly Adams and Ronald Dale (R.D.) Hott are with some of the family's Herefords on a parade float that has a sign on it advertising the Hott Herefords of Mill Creek Ranch. The Hott family was known in this area for their quality Herefords. (Courtesy of the R.D. Hott estate.)

R.D. Hott's mother, Fern Hott, is riding on a tractor at their Mill Creek Ranch with Square Top Mountain visible in the background. (Courtesy of the R.D. Hott estate.)

In this winter ranching scene, hay is being brought out on a horse-drawn sleigh to be scattered on top of the snow to feed the livestock. (Courtesy of the R.D. Hott estate.)

Big city folk do not often have pictures of themselves riding a cow as a child! (Courtesy of the R.D. Hott estate.)

This fishing trophy picture from July 1947 is similar to those found in many families' collections. Exploring the countryside and fishing were popular ways families spent their leisure time. (Courtesy of the R.D. Hott estate.)

"For the want of a nail"
A BATTLE COULD BE LOST

Your Scrap will speed Victory!

"For the want of a nail the shoe was lost
For the want of a shoe the horse was lost
For the want of a horse the rider was lost

During World War II, scrap drives were a popular way for those at home to contribute to the war effort. By donating used metal, one could help build ships and other machines needed for the war. This ad was in a 1943 copy of the *Furrow*, a John Deere magazine that was first printed in 1895 and is still in print. (Courtesy of Feather Your Nest.)

Pictured are Cub Scouts and their parents. From left to right are (first row) Tom Lines, Michael Sheridan, Gary ?, and Junior Sorenson; (second row) Harvey Catchpole, Ben L. Lynch, Leroy Mobley, and Buzzy Smith; (third row) Alva Lee Cox and David Smith; (fourth row) June Lynch, Mable Catchpole, Juju Cox, Birdie Williams, and Ms. Mobley; (fifth row) Gary's parents, Evangeline Catchpole, Hap Hughes, and Pete Mobley. In the back is the unidentified pack leader. (Courtesy of Selah Mountain Pharmacy.)

Pictured here is the 1940 high school basketball team. (Courtesy of Archuleta School District.)

The 1940 Pagosa Springs high school senior class is pictured. They are, from left to right, (first row) Mary Jane Cotton, Fred Martinez, Joe LaVarta, Sam Teeson, and Jessie Lee Smith; (second row) school superintendent Herbert Allen and sponsor Fern Barton; (third row) Ione Jacobson, Vice Pres. Gilbert Martinez, Pres. Mary Flaugh, and Louis Espinosa, secretary-treasurer. (Courtesy of Archuleta School District.)

This couple is going on a wintertime sleigh ride to enjoy the beautiful snow cover. (Courtesy of the R.D. Hott estate.)

Here are some 1940s-era Ute turkey dancers in Pagosa on the Fourth of July either before or after the parade. These types of dancers would dress up and perform at events such as parades, fairs, and intermissions during rodeos. The type of dancing was not a traditional dance that served a purpose or was part of a ceremony, but was made up for performances. (Courtesy of the Goodman family.)

This late 1940s view shows one of the towropes at Wolf Creek ski area; people are gathered on the left where skiers get on the towrope. At top right is Lobo Lookout, and the continental divide is the back ridge. A few cars on the left are on the access road loop that was on the side of Highway 160. At far right is a log shelter house that was added in 1938, and beyond that out of the picture would be the tow to Big Thunder Mountain. (Courtesy of Dean Cox.)

Sister and brother Pauline and Charles Elliot are taking a break while skiing at Wolf Creek when Charles was home on furlough from serving in World War II. Charles Elliot worked from 1936 to 1944 to develop a ski area at Wolf Creek. He and friends from Monte Vista and Pagosa built towropes and shelters, raised funds, and started a ski patrol. In 2011, he was inducted into the Colorado Ski and Snowboard Hall of Fame for his efforts in the creation of Wolf Creek ski area. (Courtesy of the Elliot family.)

Juan Gallegos and helpers have gathered the family's sheep in front of the old barn at the family ranch, which is now no longer standing. The Gallegos family is one of the many in Archuleta County that ran sheep, keeping them in the high country in the forest in the summers and bringing them down to the low country for the winters. (Courtesy of the Gallegos family.)

Juan "Junior" Gallegos II is seen washing dishes outside at his family's sheep camp. This spot is just outside town near where the historical marker is now on the side of Highway 160. (Courtesy of the Gallegos family.)

Schoolchildren are lined up outside the Stollsteimer Schoolhouse. Rural schoolhouses, including this one, were located throughout Archuleta County. Colorado's School District Reorganization Act of 1949 promoted the consolidation of the state's rural school districts into much larger districts, and after that, students were bused into towns. (Courtesy of the Gallegos family.)

The original Chimney Rock Fire Lookout Tower, seen here, was built by the Civilian Conservation Corps in 1940 and used until it was abandoned in 1957. The lookout tower was then reconstructed and opened for visitor use in 1988. The tower was taken down in 2010 because of its negative impact on viewing astronomical events, such as the major lunar standstill, which the cultural site is associated with. The area was designated Chimney Rock National Monument by proclamation of Pres. Barack Obama in 2012. (Courtesy of the San Juan National Forest.)

The marque at the Liberty Theatre is advertising that Fred Harman is coming to speak in person. The first theater operating at this location, originally constructed as part of the Archuleta Mercantile building, was a silent picture theater called the Star Theatre. After the Archuleta Mercantile building burned down in 1919 and A.T. Sullenberger built the Metropolitan Hotel building in its place, the theater was resurrected as the Liberty Theatre. The Liberty Theatre was established in 1919 and is still in operation today—it is one of Pagosa's treasures. (Courtesy of the Harman estate.)

This Sanborn postcard with a view of the main business section of downtown Pagosa was mailed in 1945. In the foreground is the Metropolitan Hotel building, which also houses a café, the Liberty Theatre, and Rickleton Drugs. Hersch's Mercantile is now a Piggly Wiggly, and the Archuleta County Courthouse is at the end of the street with Joy's Grocery Market next to it. (Author's collection.)

Seven

1950s

Seen here in front of the Hotel Pagosa in a 1950s Fourth of July parade, this past-and-present-themed float is complete with cattle. The town's ranching heritage has always been celebrated during this annual event. (Courtesy of the Harman estate.)

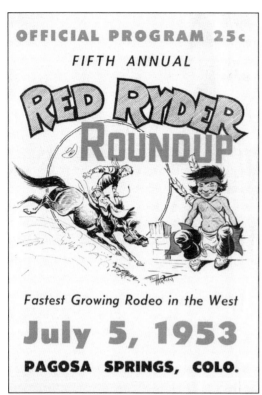

Here is the official program of the fifth annual Red Ryder Roundup from 1953. The program bills the annual event as the fastest growing rodeo in the West and features Fred Harman's artwork on the cover. (Courtesy of the Harman estate.)

This 1950s photograph shows a Red Ryder Roundup parade float decorated with cattle brands being pulled by a John Deere tractor. The Red Ryder Roundup was officially started by Fred Harman and others in 1949 when they applied to use the Red Ryder logo for the annual event. The town did have a parade on the Fourth of July prior to this, but this is what started the modern festivities of the rodeo and parade that have continued to today. (Courtesy of the Harman estate.)

Southern Ute in traditional dress are participating in the Red Ryder Roundup parade. Members of the Southern Ute Indian Tribe frequently came from Ignacio and participated at annual events in Pagosa during this time. (Courtesy of the Harman estate.)

The school marching band is participating in this 1950s Fourth of July parade. Town businesses that can be seen include Hersch's Mercantile, Pagosa Hardware, Jackish Drug, Pagosa Hotel and Café, Liberty Theatre, and Metropolitan Liquors. This is the location Ben K. Lynch moved Jackish Drug to after the original store building burned down in the 1943 fire. Other town services that can be seen in smaller signs and windows are the Continental bus station, the post office, and the telephone office. (Courtesy of the Harman estate.)

This is Miss Stampede, royalty of the Monte Vista Ski-Hi Stampede; she is lining up to participate in the Fourth of July parade in Pagosa. The Ski-Hi Stampede is Colorado's oldest professional rodeo. (Courtesy of the Harman estate.)

Passing in front of Goodman's Department store, the Cowbelles float with cowgirls is in the Fourth of July parade. Goodman's storefront is painted in its long-standing Navajo rug style, which it now no longer bears. (Courtesy of the Harman estate.)

Here is another picture of Goodman's Department Store and its painted exterior. After Louis and Hortense's son Dave Goodman came back from service in World War II, he took over the store and expanded its goods into Western wear; subsequently, the building was painted. Goodman's was one of boot-maker Tony Lama's first clients. (Courtesy of the Goodman family.)

Goodman's was one of the few places around that carried items specifically for their Native American clientele, and certainly the only store in Pagosa that did. Here, some folks are posing with their Pendleton trade blankets. Goodman's carried a wide variety of Pendleton blankets; its Native American customers wore them as shawls. The store also sold different types of shawls that catered to the tastes of their Hispanic clientele. (Courtesy of the Goodman family.)

Here, First Communion is taking place inside of the Immaculate Heart of Mary Church in Pagosa. This church, the second Catholic church to be built in town, was constructed in 1948. The first church, St. Edwards Catholic Church, was built in 1894 and burned down in the 1950s. (Courtesy of the Gallegos family.)

This c. 1958 aerial photograph was taken by pilot John C. Baird. The San Juan Lumber Mill, pictured, was opened in 1958. The Hudspeth family owned the mill and the overarching San Juan Lumber Company, which operated into the 1970s. (Courtesy of the San Juan National Forest.)

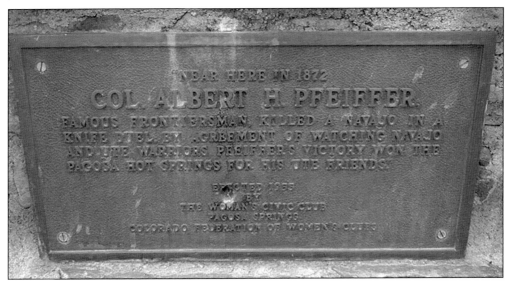

This commemorative plaque was put up on the side of Highway 160 in 1955 by the Women's Civic Club of Pagosa Springs. It commemorates a battle between the Navajo and the Ute over the hot springs in the 1800s. Though this had been traditionally Ute land, the Navajo had started claiming the springs and camping near them. The Ute chose Col. Albert Pfeiffer to represent them in a knife fight against a Navajo, whom he killed, winning the springs for the Ute. (Author's collection.)

Here, a Sno-Go is clearing the road on Wolf Creek Pass. Improved roads and winter plowing were constantly improving in the 1940s and 1950s, which helped the winter tourism and skiing economy at Wolf Creek and other ski areas throughout the state. The last section of this road was surfaced in 1950, bringing it a long way from its one-lane, dirt road inception. (Courtesy of Colorado Department of Transportation.)

Several ski spots were used in Pagosa Springs from the 1940s through the 1950s. Here are the remnants of the ski tow that was constructed in 1956 on John Masco's ranch on Snowball Road. An old truck was towed to the top of the hill and rigged to drive a rope. Poles were planted up the hill, and the rope was strung on them. The ski slope was a north-facing parabola-shaped hill about 500 yards long. The only downside to this ski hill was having to transport gas up to the top to run the truck engine. (Courtesy of Dean Cox.)

This is what Wolf Creek ski area has become known for—its powder! (Courtesy of Dean Cox.)

Pagosa Springs had a square dance club for a long time. On this parade float entry, the club members are square dancing while a band plays from the rear of the float. It is passing through what looks like downtown Fort Collins, Colorado. (Courtesy of the R.D. Hott estate.)

The American Legion Post No. 108 sponsored the town's Fourth of July rodeo from 1922 to 1948. In 1949, 40 acres were purchased from Leon Montroy to serve as the rodeo grounds, and the Red Ryder Roundup rodeo was formed. Here is the lining-up for the traditional grand entry that starts off the rodeo. (Courtesy of the Harman estate.)

The Red Ryder Roundup found its permanent location in 1950 when a fenced arena, corrals, a racetrack, a judges' stand, bucking chutes, and temporary grandstands were erected by a team of volunteers. In 1951, stables were constructed, and in 1953, bleachers were built. (Both, author's collection.)

These photographs feature the bull- and bronc-riding competitions during the 1958 Roundup. The rodeo traditionally featured bull riding, bronc riding, a cutting contest, junior calf roping, and team roping. Horse racing was also an event until it was stopped for safety reasons. (Both, author's collection.)

Here is an overview of downtown in February 1958. Former ranger John C. Baird took this low-level aerial photograph after he retired from the Forest Service. The state highway department can be seen constructing the new bridge over the San Juan River. Lois Kinser's Diner Café, fashioned from an old rail passenger car, is next to the Pagosa Bar. Citizens Bank is on the corner, and west

of it is the Moorhead Garage Conoco service station. On the left are the Catholic and Methodist churches on Lewis Street where they currently exist, and at upper right is the first Catholic church, St. Edwards, on Lewis Street, which is now gone. (Courtesy of the San Juan National Forest.)

Members of the 1953 Pagosa senior class are, from left to right, (first row) Bobby Brown, Helen Crouse, Ralph Alberico, and Minnie Belmear; (second row) Sally White, Donald LaVarta, Salle Catchpole, and Peter Stevenson; (third row) Richard Walter, Dixie Tift, and Aline Thomson; (fourth row) secretary Patsy Clark and treasurer Jerry Martinez; (fifth row) school superintendent A.D. Hahn Jr., sponsor Mrs. Gibson, Pres. Robert Smith, and Vice Pres. Wilfred Madrid. (Courtesy of Archuleta School District.)

These Pagosa Springs high school baseball team members are, from left to right, (first row) Coach McMillan, James "Jimmy" Chambers, Bob Shahan, Norman Jones, Freddy Catchpole, and Aubrey Fowler; (second row) Joe Shahan, Bobby "Bumpy" Brown, Ben L. Lynch, Leonard Kinsler, Alva Lee Cox, Charles Erdman, Junior Sorenson, Victor "Moose" Montano, and Coach Gribben. (Courtesy of the Lynch family.)

Junior prom attendees (from left to right) Ben L. Lynch, Zalma Dee "Dukie" Kingsley, Patsy McCoy, and Joe Shahan are at the school gym in 1955. (Courtesy of the Lynch family.)

The Giordano family owns the longest family-owned and -operated spa in Pagosa. They operated under the name the Spa Motel for decades, as seen here in the mid-1950s. The name was changed to the Spa @ Pagosa Springs around the turn of the century and, finally, the current Healing Waters Resort & Spa in 2009. (Courtesy of Healing Waters Resort & Spa.)

The Spa Motel opened in 1950. Similar to today, it consisted of a hotel, individual cabins, and a hot spring pool seen here with families enjoying it. Pagosa Springs's healing spring water was first used by Native Americans prior to settlement and continues in today's spas and pools. (Courtesy of Healing Waters Resort & Spa.)

Eight

FRED HARMAN

Pagosa's most famous resident, Fred Harman II, drew the *Red Ryder* comic strip for 25 years; it ran from 1938 to 1965. He was also an acclaimed Western cowboy artist. His Western cartoons, as well as his paintings, were known to show authentic action, as he had actually been a cowboy himself. (Courtesy of the Harman estate.)

In 1891, the first Fred Harman, the artist's father, homesteaded in Pagosa; this is the family homestead. The building was later moved to a collection of historic buildings at the Fred Harman Art Museum, the home of Red Ryder and Little Beaver and a rodeo, movie, and Western art and memorabilia center. Fred Harman III and his wife, Norma, opened the Fred Harman Art Museum in 1983, and after he passed away, Norma ran it through 2018. (Courtesy of the Harman estate.)

This photograph features the three brothers, Fred, Hugh, and Walker Harman. Their family moved to Pagosa when Fred was two months old, in 1902, and Walker and Hugh were born and raised in Pagosa until the family returned to Kansas City, Missouri. Fred would grow up to be a famous cartoonist and painter. Hugh is best known for being the cocreator of *Looney Tunes* and *Merrie Melodies* and creating the tagline "That's all folks." Hugh also created the 1939 antiwar cartoon *Peace on Earth*, which was nominated for both an Oscar and a Nobel Peace Prize. Walker worked with Hugh writing original cartoon series at Metro-Goldwyn but is less well known and died early at age 33. (Courtesy of the Harman estate.)

Pictured are Lola and son Fred Harman III. Lola and Fred Harman II met in St. Joseph, Missouri, when they worked in the same building, she as a musician and he as an illustrator. They married in 1927 and had son Fred III. The family moved to St. Paul, Minnesota, for a few years before buying a cabin in Harman's favorite place, Pagosa Springs. Fred struggled to keep work in the 1930s during the Depression, and the family moved several times until he basically became an overnight success when he signed a 10-year contract for the *Red Ryder* comic strip. (Courtesy of the Harman estate.)

Artist Fred Harman is at his desk at his Pagosa ranch studio. Starting when the Harmans bought a house in Albuquerque in 1951, Fred alternated between his place in New Mexico in the winter and the family ranch outside Pagosa in the summer; this was because the unpredictable winter weather in Pagosa would hamper the timely mail delivery of his comic strips. He had a studio at each location where he drew the *Red Ryder* comic strip and did his Western paintings. (Courtesy of the Harman estate.)

The family's pet deer is pictured in front of the fireplace at the Harman house. The deer liked to lay on this rug in front of the fireplace, and Lola Harman was known to play the piano for it. A photograph of the deer even made it into the back of a monthly *Red Ryder* comic book, so people around the country became acquainted with it. (Courtesy of the Harman estate.)

Fred Harman is posing with a Boy Scout troop at his Red Ryder Ranch. To separate his comic strip from others, he frequently promoted it with personal appearances and event sponsorship and was heavily involved civically. Harman even encouraged his fans to stop by his Pagosa ranch to watch him draw his comics. (Courtesy of the Harman estate.)

Here, kids are looking up at a *Red Ryder* radio show billboard advertisement. The Red Ryder franchise, which started with the comic strip, then developed into a monthly comic book, a radio show, television show, serial chapters, novels, movies, licensed products like the Daisy Red Ryder BB guns, and sponsorship of groups, events, powwows, and rodeos, like the Little Beaver Roundup Rodeo in Dulce, New Mexico. (Courtesy of the Harman estate.)

Surrounded by his comic drawings are Fred Harman and Sammy Trujillo, who played the role of Little Beaver during Fred's personal engagements when he appeared as Red. In the first episode of the *Red Ryder* comic strip, Red adopts the orphaned Navajo boy who then serves as his sidekick who was constantly saving his bacon. The character was the first true child sidekick in a comic strip, predating Batman and Robin and others by several years. (Courtesy of the Harman estate.)

Fred Harman is pictured with Sammy Trujillo, dressed as Little Beaver, in the Monte Vista Ski-Hi Stampede parade. Many children played Little Beaver over the years, including several Jicarilla Apache from Dulce. Harman appeared in events all over the country and sometimes needed backups, and when the children got older, they needed to be replaced by a new, younger sidekick. Ben Lynch remembers that a Little Beaver was needed for the parade in town one year. Someone decided that he could pass for the part as he had a tan that summer, and so a wig was put on him, and he played the role—but one time only! (Courtesy of the Harman estate.)

Fred Harman and Sammy Trujillo are seen at the horse races in Durango during the Spanish Trails Fiesta. Red Ryder and Little Beaver, Durango, Monte Vista, and Pagosa Springs' rodeo royalty and others would travel to each town's events. Durango's was the Spanish Trails Fiesta, Monte Vista had the Ski-Hi Stampede, and Pagosa had the Red Ryder Roundup. (Courtesy of the Harman estate.)

Fred and the rodeo clowns' monkey are performing at a rodeo. (Courtesy of the Harman estate.)

Fred and Lola Harman (front left) and friends are in the Blanco Basin with the Harmans' visiting friends Pop Chalee and Ed Natay. Chalee was a Taos Pueblo artist, and she and her second husband, Ed Natay, a Navajo singer, were well known in the New Mexico and Arizona art scenes. Pop Chalee's most well-known work is the series of murals she painted for the Albuquerque airport, and Ed was the first Native American artist to record an album for commercial release. (Courtesy of the Harman estate.)

Here is another image of Fred Harman II on horseback in a parade; however, this one is very different from the rest as it was taken at a parade in Tokyo. Harman was brought to Tokyo to promote publication of the *Red Ryder* books being introduced to Japan. (Courtesy of the Harman estate.)

Fred Harman is seen with a group of Japanese schoolchildren during his promotional tour of Japan. (Courtesy of the Harman estate.)

In 1965, Harman was one of the original inductees into the Cowboy Artists of America. His *Yei Bi Chei* painting of the Navajo healing ceremony of the same name was hung at the first annual exhibition at the National Cowboy Hall of Fame in Oklahoma City, Oklahoma. (Courtesy of the Harman estate.)

This is one of Harman's photographs of dancers at the Jicarilla Apache Gojiiya feast at Stone Lake on the Jicarilla reservation. It was a source of great pride for him and his family that he had the rare honor to be adopted into both the Navajo and the Jicarilla Apache tribes. (Courtesy of the Harman estate.)

BIBLIOGRAPHY

Baker, Steven G. "Juan Antonio María de Rivera." Colorado Encyclopedia. coloradoencyclopedia. org/article/juan-antonio-maría-de-rivera.

Banker, Mark T, ed. *Ferenc Morton Szasz: A Celebration and Selected Writings.* Morrisville, NC: Lulu Publishing Services, 2018.

Beaghler, Steven L. "The Automobile in Denver, 1895–1910." Master's thesis. University of Colorado, 1989.

Colorado Department of Transportation. *Welcome to Colorful Colorado: 100 Years of Colorado State Transportation History.* Denver, CO: Colorado Department of Transportation, 2010.

Jackson, A.H., ed. *The Daily Washington Law Reporter, Vol. 10.* Washington, DC: John L. Ginck, Printer, 1883.

Ladies Aide Society of the First Methodist Episcopal Church of Pagosa Springs. "Pagosa Springs Souvenir." Pagosa Springs, CO: Pagosa Springs Methodist Church, 1910.

Motter, John. *Pagosa County, the First Fifty Years.* Pagosa Springs, CO: self-published, 1984.

"Pagosa Hot Springs the Carlsbad of America." Pagosa Springs, CO: *Pagosa Springs Herald*, 1896.

Pagosa Springs Methodist Church. *100 Years of Pagosa Springs Methodists.* Pagosa Springs, CO: Pagosa Springs Methodist Church, 1996.

Pagosa Springs Sun. Pagosa Springs, CO, various editions.

Sanborn Fire Insurance Maps. Pagosa Springs, CO, 1910 and 1919.

San Juan Historical Society. *Remembrances, Vol. 1–13.* Pagosa Springs, CO: San Juan Historical Society.

Seyfarth, Jill. *Historic Buildings Survey Pagosa Springs, Colorado.* Durango, CO: Cultural Resource Planning, 2004.

Smith, Duane A. *A Time for Peace: Fort Lewis, Colorado, 1878–1891.* Boulder, CO: University Press of Colorado, 2006.

ABOUT THE AUTHOR

Author Kristin Bowen is a transplant who fell in love with the San Juan Mountains and now resides outside Bayfield, Colorado. She is an archaeologist with the Bureau of Reclamation and has previously worked for the Bureau of Land Management and the US Forest Service. She is also the author of Arcadia Publishing's Images of America: *Meeker*. Bowen received her master's degree in anthropology from the University of Montana. She is on the Register of Professional Archaeologists and is a member of the San Juan Basin Archaeological Society, the Society for Historical Archaeology, and the Society for American Archaeology. She enjoys doing public education and interpretation and sharing archaeology and history with everyone.

Discover Thousands of Local History Books
Featuring Millions of Vintage Images

Arcadia Publishing, the leading local history publisher in the United States, is committed to making history accessible and meaningful through publishing books that celebrate and preserve the heritage of America's people and places.

Find more books like this at
www.arcadiapublishing.com

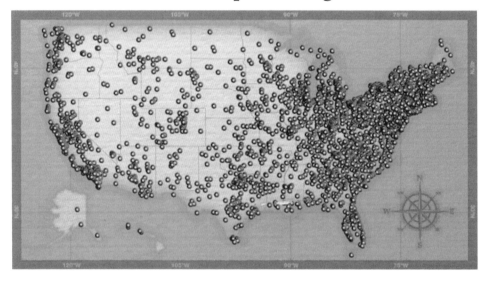

Search for your hometown history, your old stomping grounds, and even your favorite sports team.

Consistent with our mission to preserve history on a local level, this book was printed in South Carolina on American-made paper and manufactured entirely in the United States. Products carrying the accredited Forest Stewardship Council (FSC) label are printed on 100 percent FSC-certified paper.

MADE IN THE